Getting
Ready for
Our New
BABY

Getting Ready for Our New BABY

William L. Coleman

BETHANY HOUSE PUBLISHERS
MINNEAPOLIS, MINNESOTA 55438
A Division of Bethany Fellowship, Inc.

Photos are by Dick Easterday and Larry Swenson

Verses marked TLB are taken from *The Living Bible*, copyright © 1971 by
Tyndale House Publishers, Wheaton, Ill. Used by permission.

Published by Bethany House Publishers
A Division of Bethany Fellowship, Inc.
6820 Auto Club Road, Minneapolis, MN 55438

Printed in the United States of America

Library of Congress Cataloging in Publication Data
Coleman, William L.
 Getting ready for our new baby.

 1. Infants (Newborn)—Family relationships—Juvenile
literature. 2. Brothers and sisters—Juvenile literature.
3. Children—Prayer-books and devotions—English.
I. Title.
RJ251.C6   1984   646.7'8   84–432
ISBN 0–87123–295–2

Acknowledgment

Mary Coleman has made a great contribution to this volume. She has done extensive work in research, typing and editing.

Biographical Sketch

BILL COLEMAN has written half-a-dozen bestselling devotional books for this age group (three to seven) besides his very popular family devotional books for older children. His experience as a pastor, a father and a writer help to give him his special relationship with children. He and his family make their home in Aurora, Nebraska.

Contents

Some Suggestions for Parents

The arrival of a baby is usually a busy and a happy time. However, in the rush it is easy to forget about the child at home. If that child is forgotten or ignored, he frequently feels confused and displaced; the stage is set for jealousies to develop. Those jealousies could last for years.

As a loving parent there are some things you can do to make the child feel secure, loved and wanted. The following are some suggestions; I am certain you could add to them.

* Include your child in the discussions about the coming baby as early as possible. He enjoys knowing that he is important enough to be informed.

* Spend time discussing the baby and the changes which will come with his arrival. Usually you reduce uncertainty and fear by talking to a child.

* As you give information, encourage questions. Will the child lose his bed? Will the baby be there to stay? It is hard to anticipate all the questions a child might imagine; some which may seem ridiculous to an adult can be a real problem to a youngster.

* Stress how special your present child is to you and that you will have plenty of love to go around.

* Plan a happy event or purchase a gift for the child and produce these close to the time of the birth of the baby.

* Assure the child that you will have time for him. He might imagine the baby consuming all of your energies.

* Pass the word to relatives, friends and especially grandparents. When they come to see the baby, they need to give special attention to the older child also. And they should be careful not to talk only about the new baby with him. Reassurance is a key.

Some jealousy is normal and unavoidable; some will probably crop up all during their growing-up years. However, by demonstrating your love and attention, you might see brothers and sisters who care very much for each other.

Have a happy family!

William L. Coleman
Aurora, Nebraska

A Baby Is Coming!

Something exciting is going
To happen to your family.
Your parents will have
A big smile.

You will soon be as happy
As if it
Were Christmas!

Your family will get
A special present.
A small, soft, cute
Baby
Is coming to your house.

The baby will not come
To visit
But will come to stay
At your house.

Every day you will get
To see the baby
And gently touch him,
And help take care of him,
And watch the baby grow.

This baby will be more special
Than any other baby you have seen
Because *this* baby is
Your sister or your brother!

And this baby is *your* baby,
Not just the neighbor's baby.

The baby will grow up
In your house
And do things with you,
And be a special friend
Of yours.

You will be very important
To the baby
Because you are bigger
And you know more
Than the baby knows.

A baby is coming
To your house
To stay and live
With you.

You will get to know
The baby
As you grow together.
You will have
Many happy times.

You can thank God
For the baby that is coming
To your house.

**"Children are a gift from God"
(Ps. 127:3, TLB).**

Why Do Your Parents Want a Baby?

Your parents already have you.
Why do they want another child?

Let's play a guessing game.
Why do your parents want a baby?

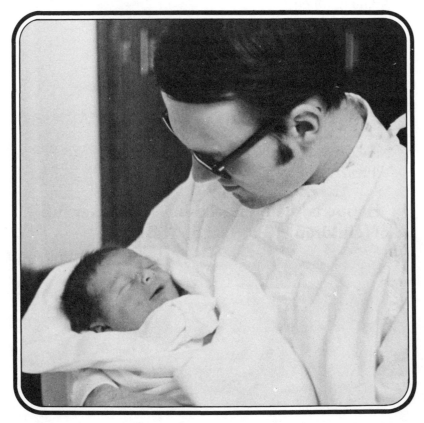

Maybe
They love you so much
They want another child
Just like you.

Maybe
They want you to have
Someone to play with
Every day.

Maybe
They want a baby,
But you aren't a baby anymore.
Now they can have
A tiny baby *and*
A big child, too.

They are glad to have
A big child like you
And a baby, too.

Let's end our guessing game.
Now you ask your parents
Why they want another baby.

**"Happy is the man who has his quiver full
of [children]" (Ps. 127:5, TLB).**

A Special Love

When the new baby
Comes to live with you,
Someone will love the baby
With a special love.

Jesus loves babies the same
As He loves children like you.

Jesus can have love
For a newborn baby
And still love you
Just as much as always.

The love that Jesus
Has for you
Never changes.

No matter how many
Babies are born,
No matter how many
Brothers and sisters
You have,
Jesus will always
Love you
Just the same.

You have a special place
In Jesus' heart
That does not change.

Lots of things change.
Your shoe size changes.

Your haircut changes.
Your favorite food
Might change.

Your room changes.
Your yard changes—
Leaves and snow fall on it;
Flowers grow.

Many things change.
But the love that
Jesus has for you
Does not change.

Jesus has a very special
Love for you.

"Then he took the children into his arms and placed his hands on their heads and he blessed them" (Mark 10:16, TLB).

Where Is the Baby?

Where does a baby live
Before you see it?
You can't buy a baby
At the store.
You can't find one
In the garden.

Babies aren't delivered
By big birds—
Such as storks.

Before a baby is born,
He lives inside
Your mother.

Many children can see
That their mother is larger
Around the waist
When a baby is living
Inside her.

But, a baby doesn't live
Inside your mother's
Stomach.
If your mother drinks
A glass of milk,
The milk doesn't
Pour on the
Baby's head!

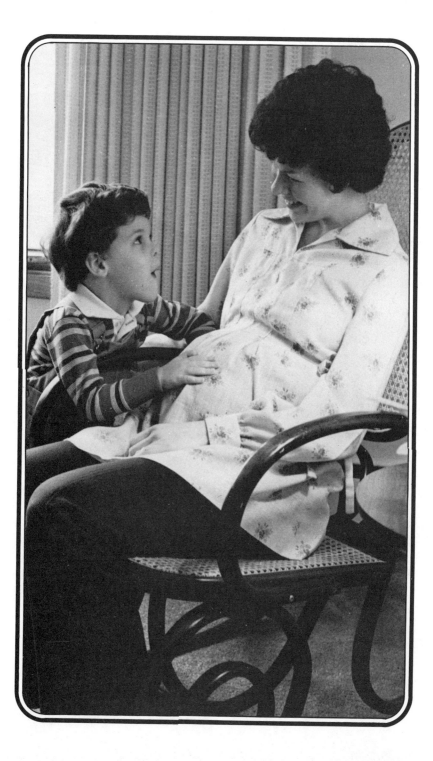

The baby has a
Special room
Inside his mother.
The room is called
A womb.

If you touch your mother,
Gently—
Where the baby's room is,
You can sometimes feel
The baby move
Inside your mother.

The baby will live there
Until he is ready
To live with you
In your house.

Ask your mother
When you will
Be able to touch her
And feel where the
Baby lives.

**"My baby moved in me for joy!"
(Luke 1:44, TLB).**

The Big Day

With all the talk
About the baby,
Your parents may have
Forgotten to tell you
When the baby will
Be born.

Parents don't usually know
The exact day,
But, they have a good guess.
It would be fun to know
And mark it on your calendar.

The baby could come
Right on the day
That Mom thinks it will,
Or it could come early
Or much later.

Sometimes babies are born
At night,
And everyone has to
Get up.

Sometimes babies are born
In the day,
And the dishes have to be
Left on the table.

Do you have a favorite
Day of the week
When you would like
The baby to be born?

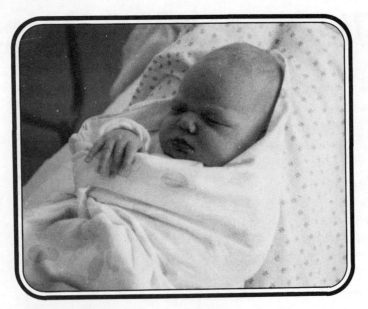

You pick the day
You would like.

What day were you born?
Maybe the baby will be born
On the same day
Of the week.

Everyone must have been happy
On the day you were born.
Your parents are so glad
They have you.
Maybe that is why they
Want another child,
Because they like you
So much.

**"You will both have great joy and gladness
at his birth, and many will rejoice with
you" (Luke 1:14, TLB).**

When Mother Goes to the Hospital

When the baby is ready
To be born,
Your mother
Will probably go to the hospital.

If your father takes your mother
To the hospital,
Who is going to take care of you?

That's an important question
And you need to find the answer.
That way you won't worry
When the time comes.

Will someone come to your house
To take care of you?
Maybe a neighbor or an aunt
Or an uncle.
Maybe your grandmother or
Your grandfather will come over.

Maybe the plan is to take you
To a friend's house or to
A neighbor.

You need an answer now
So you won't have to worry
When the time comes.

Depending on when the baby comes,
The plans might have to change.
It is good to have more than
One plan,
Just in case.

Your parents think about you
And your needs
Because they love you.

They will be happy to tell you
What the plans are and who
Will take care of you
When your mother goes to the hospital.

Be sure to ask them.

What Is a Hospital?

A hospital is a building
Where sick people go
To get better.

It is also a place
Where well people go
To stay well.

Your mother isn't sick.
But she will go to
The hospital
To give birth to
The new baby.

A few mothers have
Their babies born
At home.
Ask your mother if
She will go to the
Hospital
Or give birth
To the baby
At home.

You may have been born
In a hospital, too.
You can't remember, but
Ask your parents if
You were born in a
Hospital.

If you don't know
What the inside of
A hospital
Looks like,
Ask your parents
If you could
Visit one.

Hospitals are good places.
After the baby is born there
(Comes out of its mother),
The mother and baby
Will soon come home
To see you.

What Is a Nursery?

When someone says "nursery,"
He might be talking about
A place to grow
Baby plants.
Bushes and flowers are kept there
Until they grow bigger.

When someone says nursery,
He might be talking about
A room in the church
Where babies are taken care of
During Sunday school
Or church services.

When you were a baby,
You probably stayed in
A nursery
While your parents
Went to church.

Hospitals also have nurseries.
They are rooms where newborn babies
Are taken care of.
A nurse watches the babies
In a nursery.

Sometimes a nurse will carry
The baby from the nursery
And give the baby to its mother.

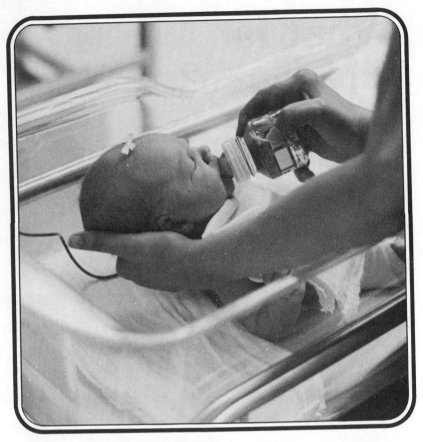

The mother will hold the baby
And feed him or change him.

The reason a baby
Stays in a nursery
Is so that the mother can rest.

If you get to see a hospital,
Stop at the nursery and see
Where your baby
Might be staying.

Doctors and Nurses

When your mother goes
To the hospital
To give birth
To the baby,
There will be doctors
And nurses there
To help both
Your mother and
The baby.

Doctors and nurses
Go to school for many years
To learn how to help
Mothers and babies.

Have you ever met
Your mother's doctor?
What is the doctor's
Name?

Is your mother's doctor
A man or a woman?
Will the nurses be
Men or women?

It makes you feel better
To know that
Doctors and nurses

Will help your mother
And your baby.

We can thank God
For doctors and nurses.

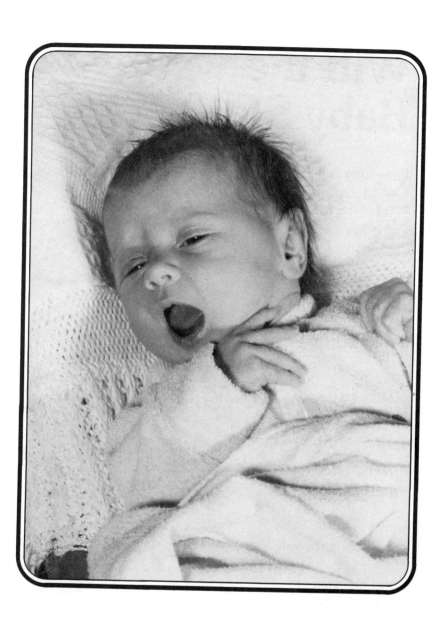

Will the Baby Stay?

How long will the baby
Live at your house?
Is he going to visit
For a week or two
And then
Live with someone else?

Is the baby going to live
With a family that doesn't
Have children?

No!
The baby is going
To come to your house
And stay.

The baby will be
Your brother or sister
And live in *your* house.

Soon the baby will
Begin to grow up
And be more fun
To play with.

As the baby grows
He will open his eyes more
And stay awake longer,
And you will have fun
Playing with him.

The baby will stay
At your house
And soon become
One of your best playmates.

A Visit From Your Grandparents

Are they coming to see you?
Are you going to see them?

Your grandparents would like
To see you
And see your baby, too.

It's fun to see your grandparents
Because they love you so much.

Do your grandparents like
To hug you or hold you
Or see your toys
Or take you to
The park?

Grandparents are special people.
Sometimes they might read to you
Or hold you on their laps
And look at pictures.

It's fun to see your grandparents
Because they love you so much.

How far away is your grandparents'
House?
Will you make a trip there or
Are they coming to your house?

What do you call your grandparents?
What do they call you?
Do your grandparents talk to you
On the telephone?

Your grandparents would like
To see you
And see the baby, too.

It's fun to see your grandparents
Because they love you so much.

The Baby's Name

Have you talked about
A name for the baby?
Maybe your parents have
Talked about it.

Ask your parents what name
They would like if the baby is a boy.
What about a name for a girl?

Your parents will choose the name
Just as they picked your name.

After they tell you
What names they
Are thinking about,
Tell your parents
Which names you
Like best.

Your parents will choose the name
Just as they picked your name,
But they would like to know
Which names you like best.

Will the Baby Look Like You?

You don't look like
A baby.
You are too old
To look like
A baby.

But if you look closely
You will probably see
A few ways that
The baby looks like you.

Look closely at the baby's chin.
Is it shaped like your chin?

Look at the baby's forehead.
Is it high or low like your forehead?

Look at the baby's eyes.
Are they the color of yours?

Often brothers and sisters
Look a lot alike.
As the baby gets older
He may look even more
Like you.

When your baby comes home,
Your parents might take a picture
Of you holding the baby.

It will be easier then to see
How much you look alike.

Brothers and sisters
Are very special
To each other.

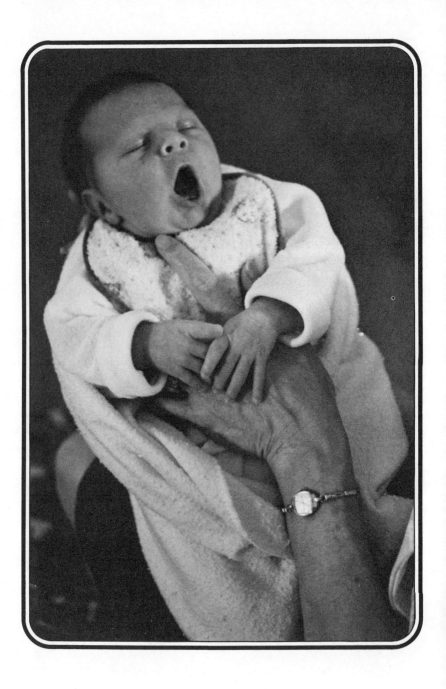

What Will Your Baby Look Like?

What will your new baby
Look like?

Will he have much hair?
Will his skin be wrinkly?
Will his nose be short,
Or long?

Will he have tiny fingers?
Will he have tiny toes?
Will the fingers and toes
Have fingernails
And toenails?

Will the baby's eyes
Be squeezed closed?
Will the baby's ears
Be small and soft?

What will your new baby
Look like?

When you see other babies
At the store,
At the neighbors',
In church or
At the playground,

Look at them carefully.
Your new baby might
Look a lot like them.

Is the Baby Adopted?

Sometimes babies become
Brothers or sisters but
They are not born
From the same mother.

Maybe your mother
Will not get big
Around the middle
Before the baby
Is born.

Maybe another mother
Will give birth to the baby,
But the baby will
Live at your house
And stay there.

The baby will still be
Your brother or sister.
We call this
"Adopting" a baby.

Ask your mother if
She will give birth
To the baby or
If she will adopt
The baby.

Many mothers adopt babies.
Babies that are adopted

Are just as loving,
Are just as much fun,
Are just as nice
As a baby
Your mother gives birth to.

Baby Moses was adopted.
One mother gave birth
To him but
Another mother
Took care of him.

A Brother or a Sister

Many of us think we know
What kind of baby we want.

Maybe we think a boy
Would be the best.
Others imagine a little girl
Would be just perfect.

But after the baby is born,
We are often surprised
How much we love the baby,
Whether it is a boy or a girl.

The baby will be much like you.
The baby will be fun to play with.
The baby will be cute and soft,
Whether it is a girl or a boy.

The baby will be special because
It will belong to you
And to your parents,
Whether it is a boy or a girl.

The baby will fit in your arms
And like to be rocked
And need to be cared for,
Whether it is a girl or a boy.

The baby will grow up
To do things with you

And go places with your family,
Whether it is a boy or a girl.

You will always be special
To the baby
Because you are older
And you know much more,
Whether it is a girl or a boy.

Every child is good
And deserves to be loved.
And you will have
Some great times
With your new sister
Or your new brother.

Will You Always Like the Baby?

Sometimes babies do things
That make us unhappy.
But that is part of being a baby.

A baby might spit up his food
And make a mess on his clothing.
A baby might cry in the night
Because he's hungry.

Sometimes babies will grab your hair
And not want to let go.
Sometimes babies will throw food
When they first learn to eat
At the table.

A baby might ruin a toy
Or a picture because he
Doesn't know how to care for things yet.

Babies can be lots of fun.
But sometimes they upset us
And we don't like what they do.

We can still like a baby,
Though we may not like everything he does.
We like our parents,
Though we may not understand
Everything they do.

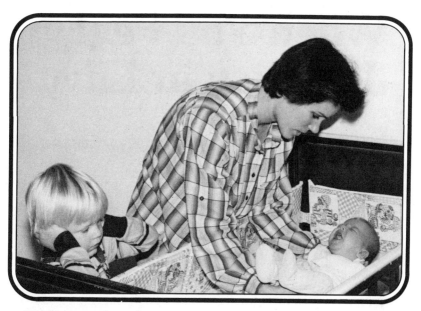

We like our friends,
Even though we don't like everything they do.

Sometime when the baby does something
That you don't like,
Remember this—
You were a baby once too!

If the baby does something wrong,
You can still love the baby.
Even though you don't like
Everything he does.

**"Let us practice loving each other, for love
comes from God" (1 John 4:7).**

When You Feel Jealousy or Envy

Envy means that we wish
We had
What someone else has.

If Amy has a red ball
And you want her red ball,
You are envious.

If Greg takes a trip
To the swimming pool
And you wish you could
Go along,
You are jealous of Greg.

Everyone
Feels jealous or envious
At some time or other.

Will you ever feel jealous
Of your new baby?
You probably will.

One day when your mother
Is holding the baby
You might think,
"I wish Mommy was
Holding me."

One day when your father
Is playing with the baby

You might think,
"I wish Daddy was
Playing with me."

That means you
Are jealous of the baby.

Later your mother
Might hold you.
Later your father
Might play with you.

There are too many
Things to do
To just stand
Around feeling
Jealous or envious.

**"Love is very patient and kind, never
jealous or envious"(1 Cor. 13:4, TLB).**

A Baby Isn't a Toy Bear

You can do
So many things
When you play with a toy bear.

You can throw a bear
High in the air.
You can drop a bear
On the floor.

You can't hurt
A toy bear.

You can squeeze a bear
As tightly as you can.
Or you can twist a bear's arm
And it won't hurt him.

You can drop a toy truck
On a bear
And the bear won't cry.

You can't hurt
A toy bear.

You can sleep with your bear,
And if you roll
On top of the bear
Your bear will be all right.

Toy bears are made of
Furry cloth and stuffing.
Their tiny eyes are sewn
Into place,
And their noses are glued on.

Your new baby
Won't be like
A toy bear.

The baby will have
Real skin and real hair.
And if he gets hurt
The baby will cry.

Babies feel the same
Way you do.
They need to be
Treated carefully.

You can't play
With a baby
The same way you play
With your toy bear.

The baby isn't like
A toy bear,
The baby is like
You.

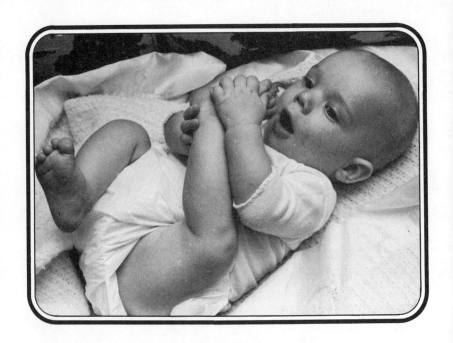

What Kind of Baby Were You?

Can you picture yourself
As a tiny baby?
Do you ever wonder
What you looked like?

Maybe your parents
Have some pictures
Of you as a baby.

How much hair did
You have?
Was your nose wrinkly?

Were your eyes closed tightly
In the picture?

Did you sit in a high chair?
Did you have a stroller so
Your parents could take you
For rides?

You probably can't remember
When you were a baby,
But you were probably
Like other babies.

You cried,
You slept,
You threw your toys,
You woke up at night,
And—
You needed to have
Your diapers changed!

People wanted to hold you.
They talked about how cute
You looked.
They bounced you on their knees
And fed you with a spoon.

You must have been
A very special baby.

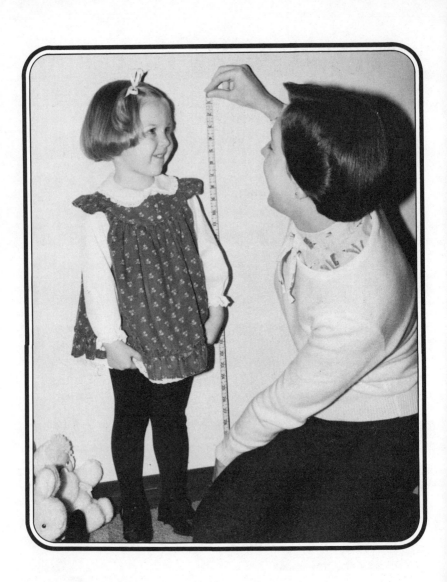

You Aren't a Baby Anymore

You must be happy
To know
You aren't a baby
Anymore.

You don't have to
Lie in
Your cradle all day
Or crawl
On the floor.

When you were a baby,
You would cry
When you were hungry.

Now you are getting
Bigger.
You are able to
Tell Mom
When you are hungry.

When you were a baby,
You had to be carried
Everywhere.

Now you are getting
Bigger,
And you can
Walk and run.

It's all right
To act like a baby
When you *are* a baby.

But you are too
Old for that now.

It will be fun
To have a baby in your home.

Because
You aren't a baby
Anymore.

**"When I was a child I spoke and thought
and reasoned as a child does"
(1 Cor. 13:11, TLB).**

Who Will Mommy Like Best?

Do you ever wonder if
Your mother will love
The baby
More than she
Loves you?

Many children wonder about this.
Maybe they were the only child
And now there are two
Or three children.

Mothers have lots of love.
They will have no trouble
Loving more than one child.

You love more than one person.
You love your mother *and* father.
(And your brothers and sisters.)

God has no trouble loving
More than one person.
God can love billions of people
All at the same time.

Sometimes your mother will
Have to spend more time
With the baby, but
That doesn't mean she loves
The baby more than you.

Babies must be fed.
Their diapers must be changed.
Babies need to be burped,
And rocked, and bathed.

But that doesn't mean
Your mother loves the baby
More than you.

Your mother has lots
Of love.
She loves you
Just as much as the new baby.

And God loves you, too.

Will Daddy Play with You?

Remember,
It takes lots of time to take care
Of a new baby.
Sometimes Daddy
Will help care for
The baby.

Babies need to be held
And played with, too.
They need to be picked up
By grandparents and
Cousins and neighbors.

But babies don't take
All of the time.
There will be plenty of time
For Daddy and Mommy
To play with you, too.

You have always had
Good times together.
Maybe you like to play
"Hide and Seek" or
"House" under the table,
Or a special game.
Maybe you like to play
Ball in the backyard.

Sometimes
You can play alone,

Because you are
Bigger than the baby.

Let your parents know
When you would like
Them to play with you.
Sometimes they will be
Too busy.
But lots of times they
Will enjoy playing with you
Just like before.

You are still very special
To your parents.

Why Do Babies Get Presents?

People get excited when babies are born.
Sometimes they have parties
And bring lots of presents.

Why do they bring presents
For a baby
They have never met?

Because it's the baby's *birth*day!
And that's a special time.
Each year you will celebrate again
On the baby's birthday.

Friends and family
Did the same thing
When you were born,
But you don't remember.

Every year your family remembers
Your birthday
And you probably have a party
And get presents.

When will your next
Birthday be?
Will you get a cake
Or ice cream
Or presents?

Birthdays are fun.

When You Feel Left Out

All of us
Feel left out, sometimes.
Parents feel left out,
Friends feel left out,
Teachers feel left out,
Brothers and sisters feel left out.

Some days *you* will
Feel left out, too.

People will talk about
The new baby.
People will look at
The baby.
People will hold
The baby.
People will sing to
The baby.
People will rock
The baby.

You might wonder if
Everything and everyone
Is for the baby.

You might wonder if
People have forgotten
About you.

Remember,

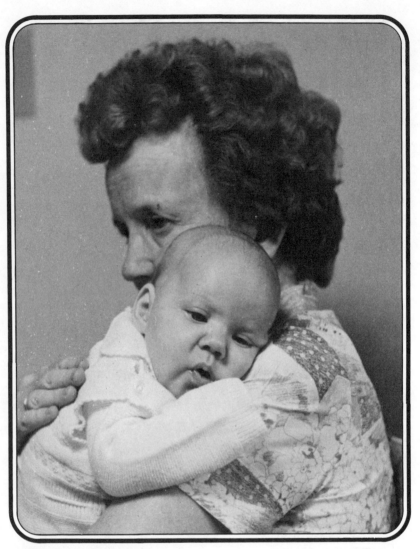

Everyone feels left out
Once in a while.

But it only lasts
For a little while.

Soon people will get used
To seeing the baby,

66

And they will begin
To spend more time
With you.

All of us
Feel left out
Once in a while.

It Isn't Fair

Have you ever had a day
When everything seemed
To go wrong?
Maybe you didn't like the lunch
Your mom served.
You got a stone in
Your shoe
Or you skinned your knee.
You dropped a big box
Of crayons
And your mother made you
Pick them all up!

Some days are awful.

And sometimes the baby
Seems to get all of
The attention.

Grown-ups stand around
Making faces and
Funny noises at
The baby.

They can sit for hours
Talking about the baby's hair,
The color of his eyes
Or his cute, new clothes.

Sometimes the baby
Seems to get all of
The attention.

It doesn't seem fair, but
Sometimes things
Aren't fair.

Be patient and see.
Before long, one of
Your parents might
Take you to the store

69

Or to the park
Or to a playground
And the baby
Won't be able to go.

Sometimes things
Don't seem fair,
But it will not
Always be that way.

"You need to keep on patiently doing God's will" (Heb. 10:36, TLB).

Look What You Have

Can you name five toys
That are yours?
Toys that roll across
The floor
Or make noises when you
Push them?

How many books do
You have?
Books with pictures
And red covers
Or yellow covers
Or green covers?

Do you have three books
Or seven books
Or do you have more?

The new baby will get
Rattles and rubber toys.
But the new baby
Can't play with most
Of your toys.

A baby can't roll a toy
Across the floor.
A baby could try to eat
Your book!

You don't have the toys
A baby has,
And
The baby doesn't have
The toys you have.

Your toys aren't right
For the baby
Because they are for a bigger child
Like you!

You don't want to be
A baby again.
There are too many things
You can do
That a baby
Cannot do.

Your Own Friends

Who are the children
You like to
Play with most?

Is there someone special
On your block
That you like?

Do you know
Someone at church
That you like?

Is there someone special
In preschool
That you like?

You probably have friends
Whom you especially like
To play with.

You must be
Happy
To have so many
Good friends.

The new baby
Doesn't have friends yet,
Because he isn't old enough.
Because you are older,
You have many friends.

Don't forget your
Baby needs you
To be his friend.

Be Gentle
with the Baby

Babies can be strong;
Babies can be weak;
Babies can be tough;
Babies can be tender—
All at the same time.

When we handle babies,
We need to know
What we can do
And what we cannot do.

You are old enough
To understand about babies.
Remember a few facts
As you touch and hold them.

A baby's head is still
Very tender on top.
Be careful not to
Bang it or poke it.

Babies will often put
Things in their mouths.
Be sure to ask your parents
Before you hand something
To the baby.

Some toys that are good
For you
Are not always good
For the baby.
Ask your parents before
You put a toy in
The baby's crib.

Babies need more sleep
Than you do.
You may have to play quietly
While the baby is asleep.

There are many things
To be careful about

With a new baby.
If you have questions,
Ask your mom or dad.

I know you
Are going to be
Gentle with your baby.
Because you are growing up.

"Be kind to each other" (Eph. 4:32, TLB).

You Can Help Care for the Baby

There will be many jobs
To do
When your baby comes
Home.

Your parents may
Like you to help
With some of the jobs.

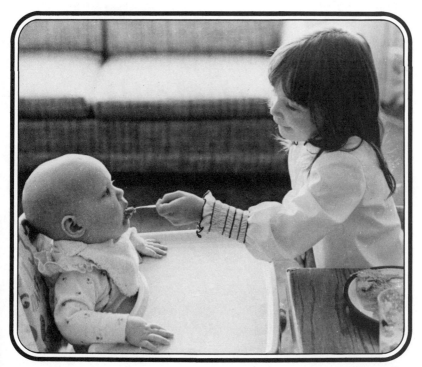

Taking care of a baby
Can be a lot
Of work.

Before you help, be sure
To ask your parents
What you should do.
And be sure you
Obey what they tell you.

Maybe they will want
You to help feed
The baby.

You might need to
Hold a bottle
Or feed the baby
With a spoon.

Maybe you can fold diapers
Or rock the baby when he cries.

You can be a big help
Caring for your new
Brother or sister.

Do You
Have a Doll?

Do you have a doll?
A special one you like
To play with?

It would be nice to
Have your doll to hold
When your new sister
Or brother
Comes home from the hospital.

Your mother will have
A new baby
And you will have
Your doll.
Both of you can
Be mommies
At the same time!

When the baby wets
And your mother
Has to change
The diaper,
You can change
The diaper for
Your doll.

When your mother talks
About her baby,
You can also talk
About your baby.

If you are a boy,
You can pretend
To be a father
Like your father.

It is fun to pretend
And do the same things
Your parents do.

Teaching the Baby

When the baby is old enough
To sit up
Without falling over,
You might enjoy sharing
A book with the baby.

A baby can't hold a book
And turn the pages
Like you can.

But sometimes the baby would
Enjoy looking at pictures.
You could tell the baby
What the pictures are.

If you give a book to the baby,
He may try to eat it
Or tear it.
A baby doesn't understand books
Like you do.

But when the baby can sit up,
The baby might like someone
Big like you
To help him look through
A book.

There are so many things
You can do
That a baby
Can't do.

The Baby Needs You

The baby won't be able
To do the things
You can do.

A baby doesn't have
Your long legs or
Your strong arms.

A baby isn't as
Tall as you are.
A baby isn't as
Fast as you are.

The baby won't be able
To do the things
You can do.

If the baby drops
A toy on the floor,
The baby will need
Someone like you
To pick it up.

If the baby kicks
The covers off,
The baby will need
Someone like you
To put them on again.
(Careful—don't cover his head!)

If the baby can't
Find his pacifier
Or teething ring,
He will need
Someone like you
To find it.

You are much bigger
Than the baby and
You can do so many
More things.

Doesn't it
Feel good to be
Grown up?

You are special
To your parents,
You are special
To your grandparents,
You are special to God, and
You are special
To the baby.

"A brother [or sister] is born to help in time of need" (Prov. 17:17, TLB).

What Do Babies Eat?

When babies are born,
They don't have
Any teeth.

They can't eat
A hot dog or
A sandwich or
A piece of chicken.

And babies don't drink
Pop or hot chocolate!

Babies drink milk, juice,
And maybe sugar water.

When they are a little older,
Babies will eat special foods
In tiny little jars,
And fine cereals
In small boxes.

But they can't chew
The things we chew.

Maybe your mother
Will let you help feed
The baby.
Be sure to ask
Before you help.

Diapers Don't Last Forever

For the first year
Or more of his life
The baby
Will wear diapers.

Babies aren't old enough to
Use the bathroom.
That is why they wear diapers.

Sometimes you might wonder if
There will always be
Diapers around the house.

But babies don't stay little forever.
They grow bigger and learn to walk
And talk and go to the bathroom
Just like you.

Diapers don't last forever.

Sometimes Baby
Will smell unpleasant,
But soon he will be clean
And smell sweet again.

Diapers don't last forever.

Some days you can help
Change the diaper,

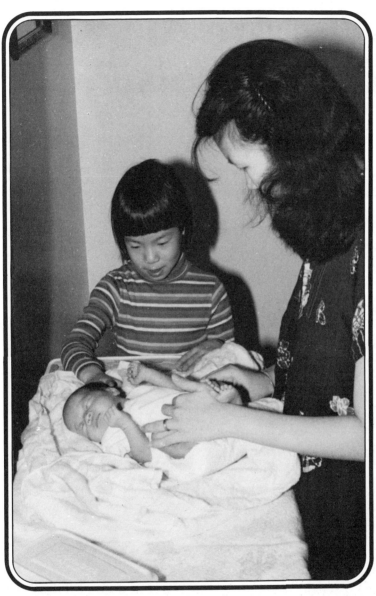

When your mother says
You can.

Aren't you glad
Diapers don't last forever?

Why Are Babies Noisy?

If a baby knew how,
He would talk to you.
Babies have a lot to say,
And they often need help.

But at first they don't know
How to talk,
So they just cry
And make noises.

When you were a baby
You cried
And made noises, too.

Sometimes a baby's noises
Are cute and funny.
At other times they are
Loud and long.

The baby has to make noise
Because he can't talk.
But, someday the baby
Will be able to put
Sounds together
And make words.

Then you and the baby
Will be able to talk together.

Many children begin talking
After their first birthday
Or before their second birthday.

Your brother or sister
May begin sooner or later.

It will be exciting
When the baby
Begins to talk.

You will enjoy
The baby even more
When you can talk together.

Where Will the Baby Sleep?

At first babies spend
A lot of their time
Just sleeping.

They like to sleep so much
They can sleep almost anywhere.

A baby will sleep on the floor
Or in someone's arms.
A baby will sleep in a basket
Or in a stroller.

A baby can sleep in the park
Or riding in a carseat.
Some babies sleep in a dresser drawer
(Open, of course)
Or on a rug.

When Jesus was born,
He slept in a stable,
Which is like a barn.

Do you ever wonder
Where you slept when
You were a baby?

A baby can sleep many places,
But a baby also needs a bed.
Will the new baby sleep
In your old crib?

Have you moved to a
Full-size bed?
You must be getting big
By now.

Ask your parents where
The baby will sleep.
And ask them where
You will sleep.

It is going to be fun
Having more children
In your house.

Chairs at the Table

When you eat breakfast,
How many chairs
Are at the table?

Will there be room
For the new baby
At your table?

At first the baby
Will probably eat
In your mother's arms.

Sometimes the baby
Will lie down
Near your table.

Babies don't need chairs
For quite a long time
After they are born.

When the baby needs
A chair,
Your parents will probably
Buy a high chair.

Maybe the baby
Will use your
Old high chair
If you are big enough
For a regular chair.

There will always be
Plenty of chairs,
Plenty of beds,
Plenty of blankets,
Plenty of food
For you
And the
New baby.

Will the Baby Be Your Friend?

Babies are too small
To be your friend right away.
But babies don't stay small
Forever.

They learn to walk
And to talk
And to play games
And to laugh
Out loud.

The baby will be able
To go to the park
Or play in the yard
Or do some of your
Favorite things.

Babies grow up
To be friends.

Before too long
The baby will be
Big enough
To play with you.

Babies grow up
To be friends.

"A true friend is always loyal"
(Prov. 17:17, TLB).

Ask Mommy
and Daddy

Do you have any questions
About the baby
That you forgot to ask?

This might be a good time
To ask.

Do you wonder where
The baby is going to sleep?

Do you wonder how many toes
A new baby has?

Do you wonder what
The baby will wear?

Do you wonder what
The baby will eat?

This might be a good time
To ask.

Do you wonder if
You can feed the baby?

Do you wonder if
You can be a babysitter?

Do you wonder how much
Babies cost?

This might be a good time
To ask.

Mothers and fathers are good
At answering questions,
But sometimes they don't know
What questions you have.

This might be a good time
To speak up and ask
Whatever you might be thinking.

Mothers and fathers are good
At answering questions.

Holding the Baby

Because you are big
And you are kind
And you are loving,
You will get to hold
The baby.

You will have to wait
Until your mother says
You can,
But you will get to hold
The baby.

You will have to sit
Up straight
In a tall chair,
And your mother will
Gently
Hand the baby to you.

Then, all by yourself
You will hold a real,
Soft, cute baby.

Have you ever held
A baby before?
If you haven't, your mother
Will teach you how.

Your mother,
Your father,
And the baby,
Each need you.

Can You Make Faces?

It's fun to
Make babies laugh.
As the baby grows
He laughs more and more.

If you can make
Funny faces and
Funny noises,
The baby will enjoy
You a lot.

Watch the faces
That others make
To get the baby to laugh.

Then you try it.
It's lots of fun.
You will probably
Be the best
Face-maker.

It's fun to
Make babies laugh.

**"A happy face means a glad heart"
(Prov. 15:13, TLB).**

Pray for the Baby

Do you pray for the people
In your family?
Do you ask God to protect
And keep them safe?

Whom do you pray for?
Do you pray for your mother?
Do you pray for your father?
Do you pray for your grandmother?
Do you pray for your grandfather?

Soon you will have a new baby
To pray for.
You could ask God to give the baby
Strong bones,
Good eyes,
Good ears.

You could ask God to keep the baby
From sickness,
From hurts,
From bumps.

You are growing up
And you can help others
By praying for them.

"Pray for each other" (James 5:16, TLB).

Sharing Clothes

Do you have any clothes
That you used when you
Were a baby?

Maybe a few blankets
Or a shirt
Or a pair of
Small booties.

Do you have a tiny hat
That won't fit you
Anymore?

The baby can't wear the clothes
You wear now.
You are too big
And your clothes are too grown-up.

Maybe you could help your mother
Collect your baby clothes
And give them to the new baby.

You will enjoy sharing
With the new baby because
You are a kind person.

It will be fun having
Your new brother or sister
Wear the clothes
That you used to wear.

"She wrapped him in a blanket and laid him in a manger" (Luke 2:7, TLB).

Who Will Watch You?

If your mother is going
To the hospital
To give birth
To the baby,
Who will watch you
While she is gone?

Remember, I asked you
This before.
Maybe no one
Has told you
Who it will be
Or maybe you
Have forgotten.

It might be your father.
It could be your grandmother.
Maybe a neighbor will come
To your house.

You might be going to spend
A few days at
Someone else's house.

Sometimes people get busy
With too much to do
And forget to tell you
Who will watch you.
Or maybe you have forgotten.

Today is a good day
To ask your parents
Who will watch you.

You Might Be Surprised

The new baby won't be able
To do the things you can do.
You are much older than
You used to be.

A baby can't chew food
Like you can.

A baby can't drink from a glass
Like you can.

A baby can't use a straw
Like you can.

You are much older than
You used to be.

A baby can't sit up
Like you can.

A baby can't pick up his toys
Like you can.

A baby can't even talk
Like you can.

You are much older than
You used to be.

A baby can't turn the television off
Like you can.

A baby can't ride a tricycle
Like you can.

It must make you feel good
To know how much you
Can do.

You will never be
A baby again.

"As Samuel grew, the Lord was with him"
(1 Sam. 3:19, TLB).

There Is Only One You

Every day there are many
Babies born.
But no matter how many
Babies are born,
There is only one you.

Babies can have
Curly hair,
Straight hair,
Wavy hair,
And almost
No hair,
But
There is only one you.

Babies can have
Pink skin,
Dark skin,
Brown skin,
Light skin,
But
There is only one you.

Babies can have
Fat cheeks,
Skinny cheeks,
Dimpled cheeks,
But
There is only one you.

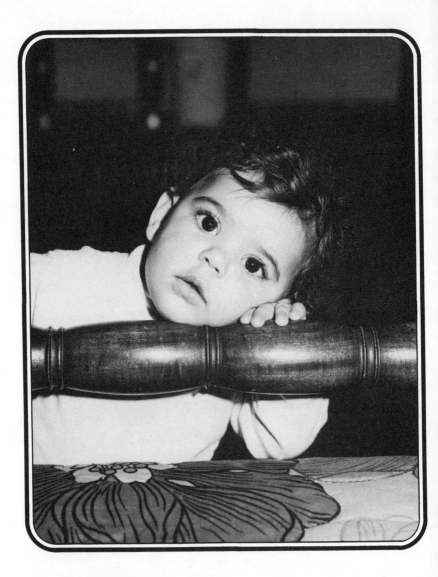

No matter how many babies
Are born,
No matter what those babies
Look like,
No one will ever take
Your place.

You are someone
Very special.
And you always
Will be.

God has a special love
Just for you,
And you have a love
For Him
That makes you
Very special.

"Because he loves us and we love him too"
(1 John 4:17, TLB).